A Mediterranean Cookbook for Kids

Rosemary Hankin

PowerKiDS
press™

New York

Published in 2014 by The Rosen Publishing Group
29 East 21st Street, New York, NY 10010

Produced for Rosen by Calcium Creative Ltd
Editor for Calcium Creative Ltd: Sarah Eason
US Editor: Sara Howell
Designer: Paul Myerscough

Picture credits: Cover: Shutterstock: Monkey Business Images. Inside: Dreamstime: Lesik Aleksandr 17b, Basphoto 9t, Bcbounders 13t, Bryan Creely 6, Elena Elisseeva 5tr, Serban Enache 5tl, Jaroslaw Grudzinski 25t, Ramzi Hachicho 21b, Tal Hayoun 21t, Lunamarina 5b, Antony Mcaulay 17t, Corina Daniela Obertas 4, Mohamed Osama 9b, Pipa100 7l, 25b, Trgowanlock 13b, Yurchyk 7r; Shutterstock: Paul Cowan 18, Dimitrios 14, Tony El-Azzi 22, Robyn Mackenzie 10, Picturepartners 26; Tudor Photography: 11, 15, 19, 23, 27.

Library of Congress Cataloging-in-Publication Data

Hankin, Rosemary.
 A Mediterranean cookbook for kids / by Rosemary Hankin.
      pages cm. — (Cooking around the world)
 Includes index.
  ISBN 978-1-4777-1339-6 (library binding) — ISBN 978-1-4777-1526-0 (pbk.) — ISBN 978-1-4777-1527-7 (6-pack)
 1. Cooking, Mediterranean—Juvenile literature. I. Title.
 TX725.M35H36 2014
 641.59'1822—dc23

                                   2013003790

Manufactured in the United States of America

CPSIA Compliance Information: Batch #S13PK8: For Further Information contact Rosen Publishing, New York, New York at 1-800-237-9932

Contents

Sea and Sunshine

The Mediterranean is a large sea between Europe and Africa. It is surrounded by the three continents of Africa, Asia, and Europe. Because it is nearly landlocked, the Mediterranean has hardly any tides and is almost a giant lake!

There are lots of countries in the Mediterranean region and they all have their own cooking styles. However, there is also a "Mediterranean" style of cooking. It is one of the healthiest ways of eating in the whole world.

Fresh food is always used in this type of cooking. Meals are based on fresh vegetables and beans, and are served with pasta, rice, and other grains. Olive oil is made locally and often poured cold over salads and breads. Fish, seafood, and chicken are cooked with lots of garlic, herbs, and **spices** to flavor the dishes. Cheeses and yogurt are also used in cooking, or they are eaten on their own.

Delicious fresh bread dipped in olive oil is eaten with many Mediterranean dishes.

The coastline of the Mediterranean is one of the most beautiful in the world.

Tuna is caught and cooked throughout the Mediterranean.

Get Set to Cook

Cooking is fun! There is nothing better than making food and then sharing it with your family and friends.

Every recipe page in this book starts with a "You Will Need" list. This is a set of **ingredients**. Be sure to collect everything on the list before you start cooking.

Look out for the "Top Tips" boxes. These have great tips to help you cook.

"Be Safe!" boxes warn you when you need to be extra careful.

Use one cutting board for meat and fish and a different cutting board for vegetables and fruit.

Always ask a grown-up if you can do some cooking.

Watch out for sharp knives! Ask a grown-up to help you with chopping and slicing.

Be sure to wash your hands before you start cooking.

Always wash any fruit and vegetables before using them.

Wear an apron to keep your clothes clean as you cook.

Always ask a grown-up for help when cooking on the stove or using the oven.

Egyptian Feasts

When you think of Egypt, you probably think about ancient Egypt. You may have learned about the pharaohs, the pyramids, and the Egyptian gods. What about the food?

Food Parties

The ancient Egyptians loved their food! We know that they enjoyed huge feasts because their wall paintings and carvings in **tombs** and **temples** show them eating lots of food.

Modern Eating

Today Egyptians eat lots of rice and bread, and they love spinach and fava beans. Fruit is also popular. Bananas, oranges, melons, peaches, plums, and grapes are all grown and eaten in Egypt, and dates are used in lots of dishes. Lamb, chicken, rabbit, and pigeon are eaten in most parts of Egypt, and fish and seafood is enjoyed along the coast.

Tea and Coffee

Egypt also has many tea and coffee houses where men meet to talk, play board games, and enjoy a delicious cup of coffee or tea.

This ancient Egyptian wall painting shows the Egyptian pharaoh Seti offering the goddess Hathor a platter of food.

Melons are one of the most popular of Egyptian fruits.

Baked Falafel

YOU WILL NEED:

1 x 15 ounce (425 g) can
   chickpeas, drained
1 small onion, finely chopped
2 garlic cloves, minced
1 tbsp fresh parsley, chopped
2 tbsp all-purpose flour
1 tsp ground coriander
1 tsp ground cumin
½ tsp baking powder
salt and ground black
   pepper, to taste
2 tbsp olive oil

Traditionally, falafel is always deep-fried. This baked version is easy to make and good for you, too! Serve in pita bread pockets with tahini sauce, and make a mixed salad to have on the side.

BE SAFE!
- Be careful when opening the can.
- Ask a grown-up to help you chop the onion and parsley.

STEP 1

Preheat the oven to 350°F (180°C). Brush a baking sheet with olive oil.

STEP 2

Put the chickpeas, onion, and garlic into a food processor and blend. Alternatively, you could mash them using a large pestle and mortar.

STEP 3

Now, add the parsley, flour, spices, and baking powder, plus 1 tbsp of the olive oil. **Season** to taste with salt and ground black pepper. Mix into a paste. Use the "pulse" button if using a food processor.

STEP 4

Shape the mixture into balls with a diameter of around 1.5 inches (4 cm). Place on the greased baking sheet. Brush with the remaining olive oil. Place in the preheated oven and bake for 20–30 minutes, turning the falafel halfway through the time.

TOP TIP   Add ¼ cup chopped fresh spinach to the mixture, if you wish.

Healthy Greece

Greece is near the center of the northern coast of the Mediterranean. It has miles and miles (km) of coastline and lots of pretty islands, too. There are many **ruins** dating back to ancient times in Greece. One of the most famous is the Acropolis, which has an amazing temple called the Parthenon.

Eating Greek Style

The Greek diet is very healthy. It includes lots of fresh ingredients and very little fat. Bread is eaten at most meals, including pitas. Olive oil is used in cooking and big, juicy Kalamata olives are eaten on their own or added to stews. The Greeks love to eat lots of fish and seafood. They use sheep and goat milk to make rich yogurt and cheese, such as feta.

Rich and Famous

Famous Greek dishes include moussaka, which is made with lamb, eggplant, and tomato with a cheese sauce topping. Spinach pie, called *spanakopita*, is popular. Stuffed grape leaves, called dolmades, are fun to make. Fillings include rice, toasted pine nuts, and fresh herbs. The fillings are put inside grape leaves, which are then rolled up and eaten. Baklavas are sweet, flaky pastries filled with nuts and honey.

The Parthenon was built on the Acropolis. It is one of the most famous sites in Greece's capital city, Athens.

Honey is often added to creamy Greek yogurt to make a tasty dessert.

Christmas Cookies

YOU WILL NEED:

For the Cookies

1½ cups corn oil

1 stick (½ cup) butter, at room temperature

zest of 2 oranges

1 cup orange juice

1 tbsp ground cinnamon

1 tbsp ground cloves

1 cup superfine sugar

6 cups all-purpose flour

½ tsp baking soda

½ tsp baking powder

1 tsp salt

2 cups finely ground semolina

¾ cup walnuts, finely chopped

For the Syrup

1½ cups superfine sugar

1½ cups Greek honey

1 cup water

There are many different Greek cookies. These cookies, called *melomakarona,* are baked around Christmas. They are almost like little cakes and are soaked in a sweet honey syrup. Share them with your friends!

BE SAFE!
- Always wear oven mitts when using the oven.
- Ask a grown-up to make and pour the syrup.

14

STEP 1

Preheat the oven to 350°F (180°C). Grease 2 baking sheets. Blend the oil, butter, zest, juice, cloves, cinnamon, and sugar in a mixing bowl.

STEP 2

Sift 1 cup of the flour with the baking soda, baking powder, and salt. Stir into the oil mixture. Add the semolina, a little at a time. Add the remaining flour, a cup at a time, to form a firm dough.

STEP 3

You will make around 40 cookies. Roll a piece of dough in your palms. Flatten and place on the baking sheets. Bake for 30 minutes.

STEP 4

Meanwhile, make the syrup by bringing the sugar, honey, and water to a boil. Cook gently for 5 minutes. Skim off any foam that forms.

STEP 5

Place the baked cookies in a large, flat dish. Pour the hot syrup over the cookies, sprinkle with the walnuts, and let them soak overnight.

TOP TIP
Try dusting your cookies with ground cinnamon before serving.

Tasty Turkey

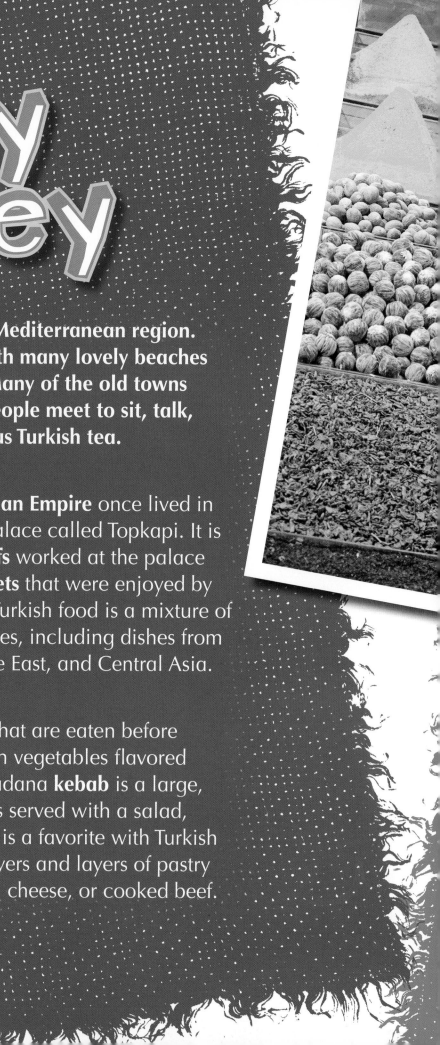

Turkey is in the eastern Mediterranean region. It is an ancient country with many lovely beaches and beautiful old towns. Many of the old towns have tea gardens where people meet to sit, talk, and enjoy a cup of delicious Turkish tea.

A Thousand Chefs

The **Sultans** of the **Ottoman Empire** once lived in Turkey. They had a great palace called Topkapi. It is said at one time 1,000 **chefs** worked at the palace to create wonderful **banquets** that were enjoyed by the Sultan and his guests! Turkish food is a mixture of many different cooking styles, including dishes from Western Europe, the Middle East, and Central Asia.

Spicy Snacks

Mezes are small snacks that are eaten before a main meal. They are often vegetables flavored with herbs and spices. An adana **kebab** is a large, lightly spiced meatball. It is served with a salad, thin bread, and rice. *Borek* is a favorite with Turkish children. It is made with layers and layers of pastry that are filled with spinach, cheese, or cooked beef.

Lots of tasty and colorful spices can be bought at Turkish markets.

Roasted bell peppers are often served as mezes.

Hummus

YOU WILL NEED:

1 x 15 ounce (425 g) can
   of chickpeas
3–5 tbsp lemon juice, to taste
1½ tbsp tahini
2 garlic cloves, minced
½ tsp salt
2 tbsp olive oil
paprika and fresh basil,
   to **garnish**

Hummus was made long ago in ancient Egyptian times. It has become a popular dish in Turkey and throughout the Mediterranean. It is enjoyed as a starter or as a snack with pita bread or raw vegetables.

BE SAFE!
• Be careful when opening the can of chickpeas.
• Ask a grown-up to cut a lemon in half for you so you can squeeze it.

18

STEP 1

Drain the chickpeas and set aside ¼ cup liquid from the can. Place the chickpeas, lemon juice, tahini, garlic, and salt in a food processor. Add the reserved liquid from the can of chickpeas. Blend for 3–5 minutes on low until thoroughly mixed and smooth. Scrape down the sides of the food processor with a plastic spatula, if needed.

STEP 2

Transfer the hummus to a serving bowl. Using a fork, roughen the surface of the hummus or make a shallow well in the center.

STEP 3

Pour the oil over the hummus or into the well. Scatter some paprika and garnish with a sprig of fresh basil. Serve with warm, toasted pita bread and vegetable slices.

TOP TIP If the mixture in the food processor is too stiff, add a little water.

Zesty Lebanon

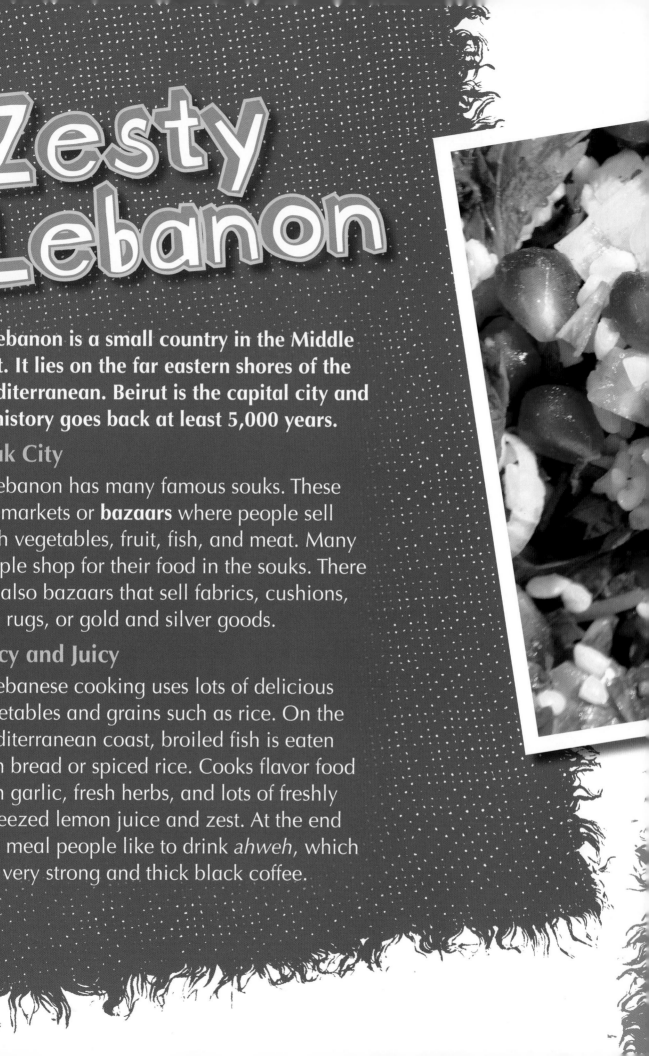

Lebanon is a small country in the Middle East. It lies on the far eastern shores of the Mediterranean. Beirut is the capital city and its history goes back at least 5,000 years.

Souk City

Lebanon has many famous souks. These are markets or **bazaars** where people sell fresh vegetables, fruit, fish, and meat. Many people shop for their food in the souks. There are also bazaars that sell fabrics, cushions, and rugs, or gold and silver goods.

Spicy and Juicy

Lebanese cooking uses lots of delicious vegetables and grains such as rice. On the Mediterranean coast, broiled fish is eaten with bread or spiced rice. Cooks flavor food with garlic, fresh herbs, and lots of freshly squeezed lemon juice and zest. At the end of a meal people like to drink *ahweh*, which is a very strong and thick black coffee.

Delicious colorful salads made of vegetables and mixed with grains and fruits are popular in Lebanon.

Mixtures of beans, nuts, and peas are used in many Lebanese dishes.

Tabbouleh

YOU WILL NEED:

1 tsp lemon zest
¼ cup lemon juice
¼ cup olive oil
¼ tsp ground black pepper
1 tsp salt
¼ cup bulgur wheat
5 ounces (141 g) flat
 leaf parsley
small bunch fresh mint
2 Lebanese cucumbers, diced
2 ripe tomatoes, diced
½ red onion, finely diced
romaine lettuce leaves,
 to serve

The main ingredient of tabbouleh is bulgur wheat. This is grown in Lebanon, along with lemons and juicy tomatoes. Lebanese cucumbers are small, and they have a lovely sweet flavor.

BE SAFE!
• Ask a grown-up to cut a lemon in half so you can squeeze it.
• A grown-up needs to chop the herbs, too.

STEP 1

Place the lemon zest, lemon juice, olive oil, ground black pepper, and salt in a mixing bowl. Whisk to combine well. Add the bulgur wheat and let it soak for 30 minutes to 2 hours. The longer you soak the mixture, the softer it becomes.

STEP 2

Wash the parsley and mint. Dry well using paper towels. Remove the lower stems of the parsley and all the mint stems. Take a handful of leaves, roll them together, and slice as thinly as possible. Then slice lengthwise so the leaves are chopped very fine.

STEP 3

Add the herbs to the bulgur wheat and stir to combine. Now add the cucumber, tomato, and onion, reserving a little of the diced tomato. Toss all the ingredients together.

STEP 4

Line a serving dish with lettuce leaves. Spoon the tabbouleh into the leaves then scatter the reserved diced tomato in the center.

TOP TIP For extra flavor, put the tabbouleh in the fridge overnight. Take out an hour before serving.

Spicy Morocco

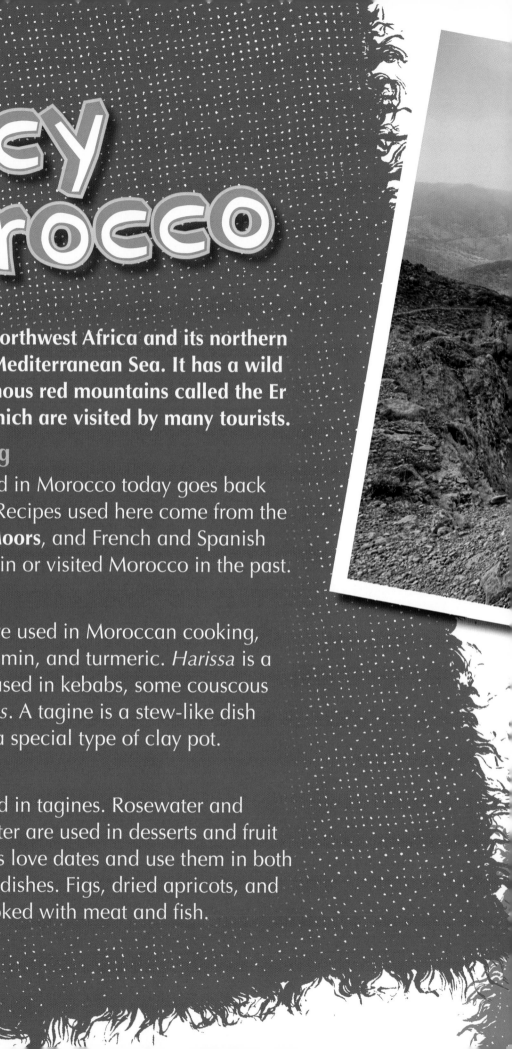

Morocco is in northwest Africa and its northern border is on the Mediterranean Sea. It has a wild coastline and famous red mountains called the Er Rif Mountains, which are visited by many tourists.

Ancient Cooking

The food cooked in Morocco today goes back to ancient times. Recipes used here come from the **Berbers**, **Arabs**, **Moors**, and French and Spanish people who lived in or visited Morocco in the past.

Hot and Spicy

Lots of spices are used in Moroccan cooking, such as cloves, cumin, and turmeric. *Harissa* is a hot sauce that is used in kebabs, some couscous dishes, and *tagines*. A tagine is a stew-like dish that is cooked in a special type of clay pot.

Fruity Flavors

Lemons are used in tagines. Rosewater and orange flower water are used in desserts and fruit drinks. Moroccans love dates and use them in both sweet and **savory** dishes. Figs, dried apricots, and prunes are all cooked with meat and fish.

Morocco's Er Rif Mountains are famous for their amazing red rock.

Tagine is cooked in a pot that has a wide, shallow cooking base and a cone-shaped top.

25

Keftas

YOU WILL NEED:

2 onions, finely chopped
2 pounds (900 g) ground lamb
fresh mint leaves, finely chopped
fresh cilantro, finely chopped
1 tbsp ginger paste
1 tbsp chili paste
2 tsp ground cumin
2 tsp ground coriander
2 tsp paprika
1 tsp cayenne pepper
2 tsp salt
4 tbsp vegetable oil
8 metal or bamboo skewers

Fun and easy to make, these lamb *keftas* are full of flavor. They can be cooked on a barbecue, under a broiler, or in a griddle pan. Serve with a tangy homemade tomato relish.

BE SAFE!
• Ask a grown-up to help you chop the onions and herbs.
• Be careful when cooking the keftas and handle the skewers wearing oven mitts.

STEP 1

Heat 2 tbsp of the oil in a pan and **sauté** the onions gently until softened. Set them aside until cool.

STEP 2

Place the lamb in a mixing bowl. Add the onions, mint, cilantro, ginger paste, and chili paste and mix. Season with the cumin, coriander, paprika, cayenne, and salt. Mix well, cover, and place in the fridge for 2 hours.

STEP 3

If using bamboo skewers, you will need to soak them in warm water for 30 minutes before using. Take one-eighth of the lamb mixture, form it into a rounded "sausage," and push a skewer through the center. Repeat to make 8 keftas.

STEP 4

Heat the broiler to high and brush with the remaining oil. Arrange the keftas on the pan. Broil for 10–12 minutes, turning occasionally, until the keftas are browned all over.

TOP TIP Leave out the chili paste and cayenne pepper if you don't like your food too spicy!

27

Mediterranean Meals on the Map!

France

Spain

Keftas

Morocco

Christmas Cookies

Now that you have discovered how to cook the delicious foods of the Mediterranean, find out where they are cooked and eaten on this map.

BLACK SEA

Hummus

Turkey

Italy

Greece

Lebanon

Mediterranean Sea

Egypt

Tabbouleh

Falafel

29

Glossary

Arabs (AR-ubz) Members of a group of people who live in southern Asia or northern Africa.

banquets (BAN-kwetz) Large meals eaten in honor of a holiday or special event.

bazaars (buh-ZARZ) Indoor markets.

Berbers (BUR-burz) Traveling tribes who live in North Africa.

chefs (SHEFS) People who are hired to cook food.

garnish (GAR-nish) To decorate food before serving.

ingredients (in-GREE-dee-untz) Different foods and seasonings that are used to make a recipe.

kebab (kuh-BAHB) A meal of roasted meat cooked on a skewer and eaten with bread.

Moors (MORS) Arab or Muslim conquerors of Spain or Portugal.

Ottoman Empire (AH-tuh-men EM-py-ur) A time in history between the fourteenth and seventeenth centuries when powerful Turkish kings ruled large parts of Europe, Asia, and Africa.

ruins (ROO-enz) The remains of very old buildings.

sauté (saw-TAY) To lightly fry food in oil or butter.

savory (SAY-vuh-ree) Food that is not sweet in taste.

season (SEE-zun) To add flavor.

spices (SPYS-ez) Powders that are rich in taste and which are used to add flavor to food.

sultans (SUL-tinz) Turkish kings.

temples (TEM-pelz) Places where people go to worship.

tomb (TOOM) A stone building in which bodies are buried.

Further Reading

Behnke, Alison. *Cooking the Mediterranean Way*. Easy Menu Ethnic Cookbooks. Minneapolis, MN: Lerner Publishing Group, 2005.

Jackson, Elaine. *Discover Turkey*. Discover Countries. New York: PowerKids Press, 2012.

Sheen, Barbara. *Foods of Greece*. Taste of Culture. Farmington Hills, MI: Kidhaven Press, 2005.

Websites

Due to the changing nature of Internet links, PowerKids Press has developed an online list of websites related to the subject of this book. This site is updated regularly. Please use this link to access the list: www.powerkidslinks.com/caw/medi

Index